My Kiss Won't Miss

Lesley Rieland
Illustrated by Mirela Tufan

My Kiss Won't Miss
Written by Lesley Rieland
Ilustrated by Mirela Tufan

2nd Edition

All rights reserved, including the right of reproduction
in whole or in part in any form.

Published by Seraph Creative 2020
ISBN: 978-1-922428-07-3

*For my daughters, Christina and Katelyn.
And for all children, that they may know the love of God
Who reconciles us unto Himself
L.R.*

Night draws near.
The sun can't stay.

Rest now, my Love. Don't run away!

If you should find a place to hide,
Then I will seek you far and wide.

I'll search for you both high and low.
Where did my Beloved go?

Yes... if I can't catch you for a kiss, I'll *blow* a kiss, and it won't miss!

In beds of flowers by blue streams

My kiss will find you in your dreams.

In blankets made of snowflake lace
My kiss will come and warm your face.

If I can't catch you for a kiss,
I'll *blow* a kiss and it won't miss!

The clouds may hide you in the sky
But you should know, my kisses *fly*!

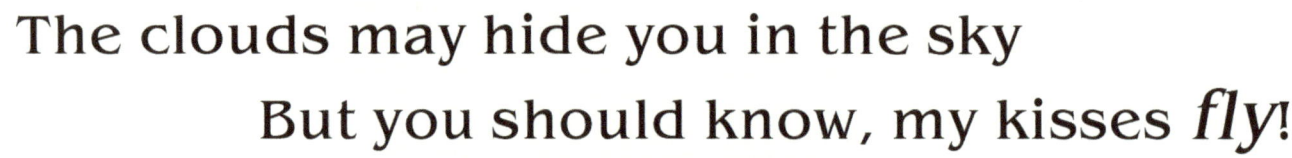

If I can't catch you for a kiss,
I'll *blow* a kiss and it won't miss!

If nestled in a cozy cave,

Or lulled to sleep on gentle wave,

If on the ocean bed you sleep

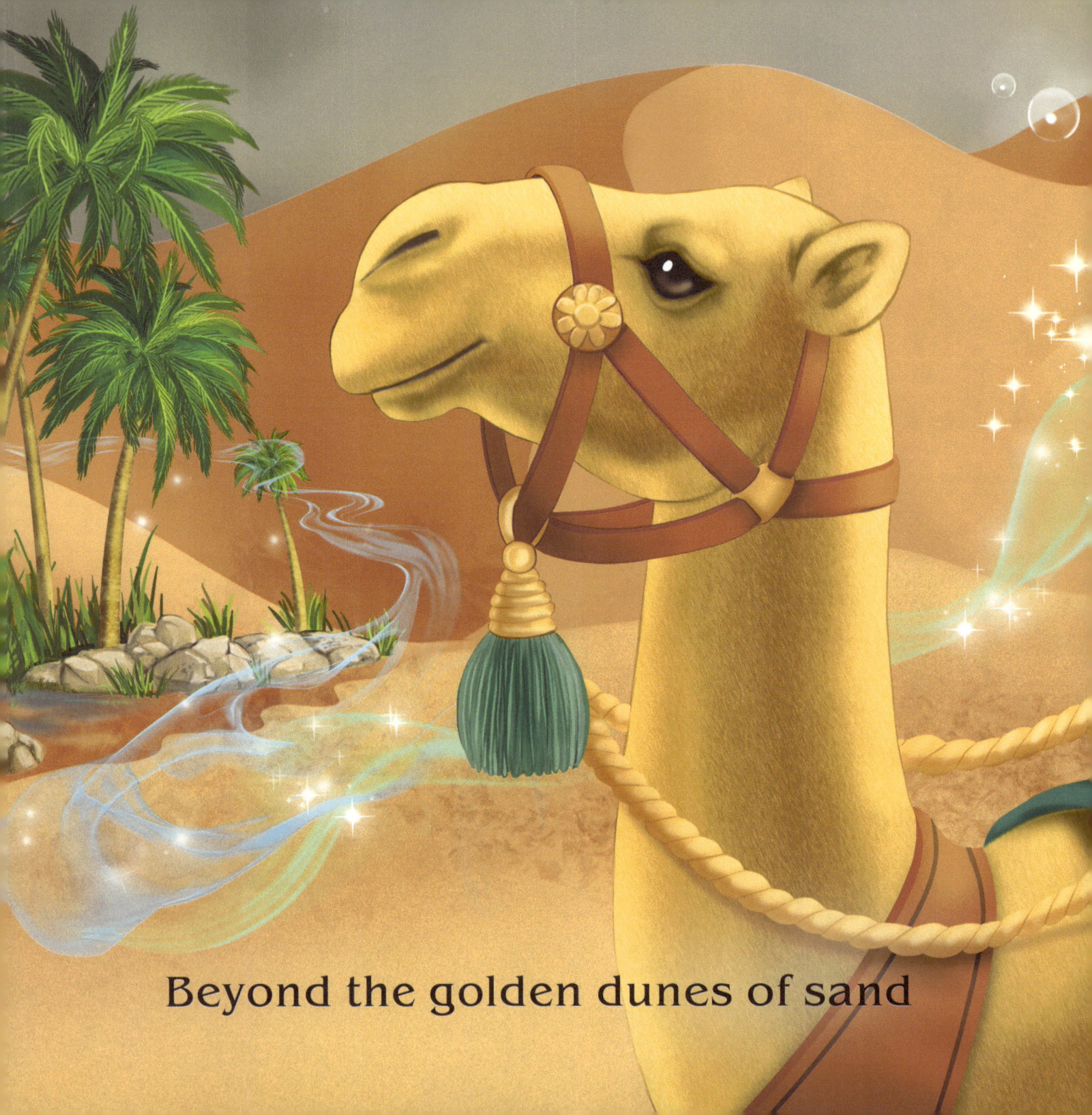
Beyond the golden dunes of sand

My kiss will search throughout the land.

My kiss will scale up mountaintops.
It rides a wind that *never* stops.

It doesn't matter where you are
I'll blow my kiss there from afar.

So snuggle softly in your bed.
Close your eyes and rest your head.

Tuck-tuck now. Out goes the light.
Now in your dreams throughout the night...

The Lord will send His goodnight kiss.

www.ingramcontent.com/pod-product-compliance
Lightning Source LLC
Chambersburg PA
CBHW050758110526
44588CB00002B/42